Handbook
for
Today's
Catechist

- ∾ *The role of the catechist*
- ∾ *Planning effective lessons*
- ∾ *Sharing the faith*

GINGER INFANTINO

Liguori

ONE LIGUORI DRIVE
LIGUORI MO 63057-9999

Imprimi Potest:
Thomas D. Picton, C.Ss.R.
Provincial, Denver Province
The Redemptorists

Imprimatur:
Most Reverend Robert J. Hermann
Auxiliary Bishop, Archdiocese of St. Louis

Published by Liguori Publications
Liguori, Missouri
To order, call 800-325-9521
www.liguori.org

Copyright © 2009, Ginger Infantino

Library of Congress Cataloging-in-Publication Data

Infantino, Ginger.
  Handbook for today's catechist : the role of the catechist : planning effective lessons, sharing the faith / Ginger Infantino.
     p. cm.
  Includes bibliographical references.
  ISBN 978-0-7648-1846-2
  1. Catechists—Handbooks, manuals, etc. 2. Catechetics—Catholic Church—Study and teaching. 3. Catholic Church—Education—Handbooks, manuals, etc. 4. Christian education—Handbooks, manuals, etc. I. Title.
  BX1968.I595 2009
  268'.82--dc22

                                                                    2009020879

Copyright acknowledgments are at page 7.

Liguori Publications, a nonprofit corporation, is an apostolate of the Redemptorists. To learn more about the Redemptorists, visit Redemptorists.com.

Printed in the United States of America
13 12 11 10   5 4 3

CONTENTS

ACKNOWLEDGMENTS

This work would not have been possible without the love and support of Bob, my husband and soul mate of forty-seven years. He has encouraged my ministry every step of the way, took on many additional responsibilities when I became involved in diocesan ministry, and used his exceptional talents as an education professor to diligently proofread and make suggestions for this publication. Bob is a great inspiration and witness of what it means to be an active, involved Christian.

I am grateful to our six children, Bob, Susan, Debbie, Karen, Amy, and Paul, and also to our grandchildren for their encouragement and excitement at having Mom and Grandma take on the additional role of author. Special thanks to Paul for the Tuesday afternoon pep talks!

Many thanks to my "groupies": Georgia, Sandy, Sharon, Judy, and Yolanda—who pray and share faith with me each week, but who especially prayed me through this writing period.

I am also deeply appreciative to the thousands of catechists in the Diocese of San Diego who participated in catechist certification courses, workshops, and classes that I developed in my thirty years as the diocesan director. Their "yes" to the ministry of catechesis, their desire to learn more about their faith, and their willingness to share faith with others have provided the inspiration and foundation for this publication.

Special thanks to Father Mat Kessler and Liguori Publications for giving me the opportunity to share my catechetical experience, and especially to Ron Knapp for walking me through the publication process with humor and enthusiasm.

SOURCES AND PERMISSIONS

Reprinted with Permission:

Additional Resources:

Pope John Paul II. *Apostolic Exhortation On Catechesis in Our Time.* 1979. Retrieved April 2009 from http://www.vatican.va.

Pope Paul VI. *Apostolic Exhortation On Evangelization in the Modern World.* 1975. Retrieved April 2009 from http://www.vatican.va.

Santa, Thomas M., C.Ss.R. *The Essential Catholic Handbook of the Sacraments.* Liguori, MO: Liguori Publications, 2001.

To Teach as Jesus Did, A Pastoral Message on Catholic Education. Washington, DC: United States Conference of Catholic Bishops, 1972.

1

CALLED TO BE A CATECHIST

The National Archives in Washington, D.C., provides visitors with an extraordinary opportunity to be in close proximity to treasured objects from the tradition, culture, and history of the United States. Once patrons navigate the electronic screenings and bag searches, they are invited to read about and to view the invaluable treasures, original documents, and precious heirlooms that comprise the history and traditions of our country. Some of these precious treasures are heavily guarded and secured under glass. Any attempt to get too close or to touch these priceless holdings will set alarms ringing and guards running.

You have been called to be a catechist, entrusted with a privileged ministry. You have been called to hand on the precious treasure of the Catholic faith to countless young people. This priceless gift of faith is not like the static, lifeless museum pieces that can only be read about and viewed through glass barriers. The treasure which you hand on is the living and active faith, passed down from the time of the Apostles until now. This incorruptible treasure is meant to be experienced, shared, and spread as good news for all people. This living, dynamic gift of faith is meant to be touched and to touch.

In responding to the call to be a catechist, you are not alone; you join hundreds of thousands of committed Catholics who have answered the call to serve. You have responded to the call because you love the Lord Jesus and you desire to share that love with young people. Perhaps your call was not as dramatic as the call to Moses from a burning bush, or as astounding as the call to Paul, who was knocked from his horse, or as life-changing as the call to Peter, who was asked to leave his livelihood. Your call may have come from a conversation with the parish director or from a flicker of interest as you read a bulletin announcement containing the annual request for catechists.

The manner in which you received the call is not important. What is important is that you have said "yes." That tiny yes has very grand implications. In giving that yes, you are responding to your baptismal call to be a disciple, to follow Christ, and to teach in his name. Pledging to use your gifts and talents to lead others to Christ, you answered the interior call of the Holy Spirit to serve in a specific ministry in the Church (see *National Directory for Catechesis*, hereafter *NDC,* 228).

There is no reason to be fearful or afraid to accept this call and responsibility. You can trust the Holy Spirit for inspiration; you can look to Jesus, the model teacher, for guidance; you can rely on your parish director for assistance; and you can count on experienced catechists at your parish for support.

A word about terminology: the term "catechesis" is the word used by the early Church to express how it handed on the teachings of Jesus and the faith of the Church. It comes from the Greek word *catechein*, which means "to echo." Catechists are those who echo the teachings of Jesus and the faith of his Church and hand them on to believers.

As a catechist, you are tasked with communicating God's message in its entirety and in fidelity to Church teaching, so you want to be as prepared as possible to take on this ministry. Basic formation courses, workshops, and conferences will increase your knowledge and skills. Catechist meetings will provide necessary information regarding the parish curriculum, guidelines, and procedures. Such meetings also offer opportunities to meet other catechists and to share information and ideas.

Catechists Participate in an Ecclesial or Church Ministry

Catechists accept an important role in the evangelizing and catechizing efforts of the Church as they are called and sent by the Church to hand on the faith of the Church (see *NDC* 241–242). Since catechists serve in an ecclesial or Church ministry, they must be practicing Catholics who live a life that is consistent with Church teaching (see *NDC* 228–229). They possess a personal commitment to Jesus Christ as the center of their lives, and they strive to strengthen that commitment through an active prayer life. Catechists demonstrate their deep love for the Church through active participation in its liturgical life. Catechists are committed to teach in the Roman Catholic tradition and to participate in the community life of the parish. They are faith-filled persons who have a strong awareness of God's presence in their lives and who witness to that presence in word and example.

Since catechists serve in a Church ministry that involves minors, they are screened and are required to participate in safe environment training. Catechists willingly comply with these regulations because they understand the importance of protecting children and providing a safe environment where young people can learn.

Jesus the Model Teacher and Catechist

Jesus Christ is the teacher and catechist par excellence. When the American bishops issued a pastoral message on Catholic education, they titled it *To Teach As Jesus Did* (1972). This intriguing title provides both a mandate for catechists to fulfill and a goal to which catechists can aspire. Jesus the model teacher provides a model and example for all catechists.

Jesus the teacher knew his material well, and he spoke and taught with authority. He understood the Hebrew Scriptures and taught his listeners about the great love, forgiveness, and compassion of God, his Father. Jesus knew his audience and taught them according to their needs. After teaching the crowds, Jesus gave his disciples more in-depth instruction on points they misunderstood. He was an excellent storyteller who often used parables to teach the mysteries of the kingdom. Jesus used questions to probe the hearts and minds of those he encountered; he was gentle with those who genuinely sought answers. But Jesus did not hesitate to debate with persons who were hypocritical or cynical—he often answered their tricky questions with challenging new questions that left them speechless.

Jesus used simple examples from the everyday experience of the people to teach deep truths. His catechetical toolbox included the birds of the field, sheep, shepherds, coins with Caesar's imprint, the tears of a woman, fish, fishing nets, lamps, lamp stands, seeds, trees, grass, water, yeast, bread, vineyards, and wine. Jesus did not confine his teaching to the walls of the synagogue. The world was his classroom, and he made use of every opportunity to teach—weddings, funerals, crowded hillsides, deserted places, well-traveled roads, stormy seas, public gatherings, and private dinners. Jesus was sensitive to people's needs and taught about the kingdom through miracles, healings, and exorcisms. He went beyond the taboos of his time; he touched the untouchable, he spoke with women deemed unclean, he welcomed the marginalized, and he ate with sinners.

In the time of Jesus, students chose the teachers under whom they would study. But Jesus chose his own students to teach and to apprentice. Jesus was a charismatic leader—with just a few words of invitation, his disciples left their families and their work and followed him. He often sought seclusion in order to pray and nourish his relationship with his Father. Jesus taught his disciples to pray and to call God their Father. For three years, he explained the mysteries of the kingdom to his disciples. Jesus modeled ministry for them, he entrusted them with his own mission, and finally he sent them out to continue that mission.

Jesus did not choose perfect disciples to accomplish the monumental work of the kingdom. The synoptic Gospels portray a rather dismal and embarrassing picture of the rag-tag group of disciples Jesus called. They consistently misunderstood the message and needed it repeated over and over again. The disciples asked for high places in the kingdom; they were afraid and lacked trust. One of these chosen disciples betrayed Jesus, and others denied him and abandoned him at his most difficult hour. Yet Jesus chose them, he forgave them, and he continued to work with them. Jesus molded these weak and insecure disciples into the small but powerful group of leaders who would go out and change the world.

Even though you may achieve marvelous results with young people, you are not expected to be a miracle worker! However, you are expected to be an effective communicator of the message. Allowing Jesus, the model teacher, to mentor you can increase your effectiveness. Following his approach, you will learn about your students, their diverse backgrounds, and their individual needs. You will use examples from their everyday experiences to teach the truths of the faith and to relate those truths to their lives. You will answer questions and repeat the message until it is clear. There will be times when you will abandon a prepared lesson in order to bring love, forgiveness, or compassion to a situation. You will teach young people how to pray and how to be disciples, and you will be challenged to be an example of what it means to be a Christian.

In accepting the call to be a catechist, you will strive to increase your knowledge of the teachings of the Church and to grow in your understanding of how to hand on the precious treasure of the living faith. You will learn more and more about Jesus, your mentor and your model. You will deepen your own call and your commitment to follow Jesus Christ who "…is at once the message, the messenger, the purpose of the message, and the consummation of the message" (*NDC* 4).

2

FOUNDATIONAL PRINCIPLES OF CATECHESIS

As a catechist, you want to be aware of some basic and foundational principles that influence the ministry of catechesis. These principles are culled from recent Church documents, provide guidance and direction for catechetical ministry, and offer valuable background information for catechists. But these documents are not intended for direct use with children. Three important catechetical documents provide the basis for the principles of catechesis and are referred to throughout this catechist handbook:

○ The *Catechism of the Catholic Church (CCC),* published in 1994, is a compendium of the faith organized in four parts: the Creed, the sacraments, the life of faith, and prayer.
○ The *National Directory for Catechesis (NDC),* published in 2005, provides diocesan and parish leadership with guidelines and standards for catechesis in the United States.
○ The *United States Catholic Catechism for Adults (USCCA)*, published in 2006 and based on the *Catechism of the Catholic Church*, consists of stories, doctrinal teachings,

applications, prayers, and reflection questions in an easy to read format.

The principles of catechesis that are listed below shape catechist formation programs, parish catechesis for children and adults, and all recent catechetical publications.

Principle One:
Catechesis Is a Lifelong Process

The ultimate object of all our catechesis is intimacy and communion with Jesus Christ (see *NDC* 55). Catechesis is much more than elementary religious education; it is a process of lifelong learning and formation for discipleship. Catechesis begins at birth and extends throughout the life cycle. Adult faith formation is a catechetical priority because only adults have the capacity to make a mature response (see *NDC* 187).

Principle Two:
Catechesis Is a Work of Evangelization

From its earliest beginnings, the Church responded to the missionary mandate given by Christ (see Matthew 28:18). That mandate commissioned the early Church, and the Church of today, to go out, to make disciples, to baptize, and to teach. Pope Paul VI stated that it is the Church's "deepest identity" to evangelize: "She exists in order to evangelize" (Pope Paul VI, no. 14). This mandate calls all Christians to be evangelists, to go into their everyday environments—family, work, social—to bring Christ to those environments, and to bring those environments to Christ. This mandate comes with a promise. No disciple takes on this mission alone; disciples are promised the gift of the Holy Spirit as they carry out their work.

Pope John Paul II described catechesis as an "essential moment" in the evangelization process (Pope John Paul II, no. 18). Catechesis has an important and particular role in carrying out the missionary mandate of the Church. Catechesis seeks to "make evangelizers of those who have been evangelized" (*NDC* 51; *General Directory for Catechesis* 58).

Principle Three: Catechesis Has Six Tasks

At its foundation, catechesis is about forming disciples who know the faith and Tradition; who celebrate the faith through prayer, liturgy, and the sacraments; who live their faith through service; and who pass on the faith to others. The six tasks of catechesis set forth in the *National Directory for Catechesis* (60–63) can be summarized as follows:

○ Communicate the message: catechesis instills a love of Christ and his teachings. Disciples who love Christ want to know Christ more fully and hand on his teachings.

○ Celebrate Christ's presence in liturgy and sacraments: catechesis teaches those who know and love Christ how to celebrate his saving presence in liturgy and in the sacraments, especially in the Eucharist.

○ Foster conversion: catechesis promotes moral formation and conscience formation. Disciples embrace Christ's values and attitudes and use them to make decisions to live a moral life.

○ Encourage communion: catechesis fosters a spirit of prayer and relationship. Disciples strive to deepen their personal relationships with Christ.

○ Nurture community: catechesis cultivates a community of disciples and prepares them to participate in the life and mission of Christ.

○ Prepare missionaries: catechesis implants an evangelizing spirit that motivates disciples to spread the Good News as Christians living in society.

Principle Four:
The Bishop Is the Chief Catechist
of the Diocese

The ultimate responsibility for handing on the faith rests with the local bishop, who makes certain that the faith is handed on in a way that is complete and accurate. He ensures that the criteria for authentic catechesis, as presented in the *National Directory for Catechesis* (75), are adhered to in catechist formation courses, in catechetical programs, and in catechetical textbooks selected for use by parishes.

Principle Five:
Lay Christians Have Specific
Roles in Catechesis

By virtue of their baptism, all Christians are called to participate in the mission of the Church to evangelize and catechize. While all share in the task of spreading the Gospel and witnessing to Christ in words and action, some have more specific roles in the formation of children. Parents, catechists, and the parish community share the responsibility for the catechetical formation of children. Each has a role in witnessing to the faith, in transmitting the faith, and in providing an environment where faith is experienced.

THE ROLE OF PARENTS

Parents are the primary educators of their children; they are the first and most influential catechists. The catechesis that happens within the family is usually "caught" rather than taught. It is spontaneous and responds to situations and experiences as they arise within the family. Parents are always teaching, even if they are unaware of it.

Parents foster Christian values and virtuous living in their children beginning at an early age. They have a serious responsibility to nourish the faith life of their children. "Their faith, their attitude toward other human beings, and their trust in a loving God strongly influence the development of the child's faith. Parents are catechists precisely because they are parents. Their role in the formation of Christian values in their children is irreplaceable" (*NDC* 203).

Parishes provide assistance to parents in carrying out their responsibility. Parishes offer pre-baptismal sessions for parents and stress the important role of parents in shaping the religious beliefs and practices of their children. Many parishes offer workshops or discussion groups on parenting and encourage parents to participate in adult formation opportunities. Most parishes provide materials and guidance to parents to help them prepare their children for the sacraments. Many parishes have programs that reach out to parents who may be separated from the Church and guide them in taking the necessary steps to return to active sacramental life.

THE ROLE OF THE CATECHIST

Catechists have a particular and specific role in the catechesis of children and young people. They are responsible for systematic and intentional catechesis. This systematic catechesis is amplified each year, leading young people into a deeper relationship with the Lord Jesus and with his Church. Catechists hand on the faith in an intentional manner, using the curriculum that is selected by the parish.

THE ROLE OF THE PARISH COMMUNITY

The parish community also has a catechetical role—to witness to young people. It provides an example of what a mature Christian community is and how it functions as the Body of Christ. The parish invites young people to be involved in and to experience a faith community in action. The parish demonstrates how the community continues to learn and grow in faith and in spirituality, how it prays and worships through liturgy and sacraments, and how it carries on the mission and ministry of Jesus through service.

Principle Six:
Catechesis Is Adapted to the Age
and Stage of the Learner

Catechesis makes use of a common language and common formulas to hand on the teachings of the faith. As a Church, "We do not believe in formulas, but in those realities they express, which faith allows us to touch" (*CCC* 170). Catechesis uses language and methods that are suited to the age and stage of development of the learners and takes into consideration their cultural backgrounds, life situations, and special needs without altering "...the substance of faith" (*NDC* 87).

It is important for you to be familiar with these principles and to understand their influence on the catechetical process. If you have a basic grasp of the material that you teach and if you use the parish curriculum, you will see that these foundational principles are integrated into your formation courses, your catechist manual, and the student materials. An understanding of these principles will help you to plan and prepare your lessons.

3

PLANNING AND PREPARING LESSONS

Making a first-time trip to a distant destination can be exciting and exhilarating, but also a bit daunting! Plans are made well in advance—collecting information from tour books, mapping the itinerary, securing airlines and hotels, deciding how much money to spend. Most travelers try to be as organized as possible so they can really enjoy the excursion.

A similar scenario holds true for catechesis. As a catechist, you are about to embark on an awesome adventure. You will accompany a group of young people on a journey of faith where they will meet the Lord Jesus, listen to his teachings, be invited to follow Jesus as disciples, and learn about the Church and its mission. As with any major excursion, you do not want to leave the details of this journey to chance; you want to be as organized as possible and plan as much as you can so that you are able to enjoy this remarkable journey along with your students.

Advance Planning: The Remote Preparation

The first step in advance planning is to become familiar with your catechist manual or the teacher guide that accompanies the student textbook. This great resource is an indispensable tool that guides your teaching, provides doctrinal preparation, and suggests many methods and activities. Set aside a couple of hours for this remote preparation and use a notebook to jot down notes and important details.

Begin this remote preparation—as you will begin all planning and preparing—with a prayer to the Holy Spirit for openness, for wisdom, and for understanding. Pray also for the students whom the Lord will send you to teach. Next, relax and browse through your manual. Review the table of contents and notice the major doctrinal concepts for this grade. Skim the book to get a sense of how information in the manual is organized. Every textbook series is different, but most catechist manuals include:

○ a scope and sequence chart that demonstrates the entire curriculum for grades one through eight and synthesizes how the textbook series presents the systematic catechesis that all students should receive.
○ a profile of students that includes psychological, cognitive, and faith development characteristics.
○ background information for the catechist on the doctrinal concepts to be taught.
○ a copy of the student text within the pages of the manual.
○ lesson plans for each session to include step-by-step instructions on how to teach the lesson, additional activities to support the lesson, and audio-visual possibilities.

Some series also provide:

○ Internet support for lessons.
○ reproducible blackline masters.
○ family pages to send home.
○ assessment tools.

As you get a sense of the subject matter for the coming year, you may need to increase your own understanding of the material through further reading or study. For example, if you are teaching eighth grade with its theological focus on the Creed, you may want to review the *Catechism of the Catholic Church,* Part One: The Profession of Faith (26–1065); if you are teaching fifth grade with its concentration on the sacraments, you may want to read *The Essential Catholic Handbook of the Sacraments* (Liguori Publications, 2001).

This type of remote planning also allows you to make preparations for out-of-classroom activities. For example, if you wish to bring your sixth graders to a Jewish temple since they will study the Old Testament, prior arrangements need to be made for the tour, transportation, and parent permission.

A Brief Profile of the Students and Their Curriculum

As you plan lessons, be aware of the profile of the students you teach and how the curriculum responds to their stage of development.

Primary students live in a world centered on themselves, their homes, and their families. Their world is broadening as they participate in school, church, sports, and other activities. These youngsters have short attention spans. Catechists need to balance movement with quiet time, and listening activities with "doing" activities. These very concrete learners respond to sensory activities and examples from the real world. They like hands-on activities, as well as story, song, gesture, and surprise.

In the primary curriculum, students uncover God's love for them as it is expressed in creation and in God sending his Son, Jesus. They hear stories of how Jesus lived, and they are invited to develop a personal relationship with Jesus, who leads them to the Father. Students are introduced to the Holy Spirit, who forms and guides the Church, the community of believers. Most students will celebrate their first penance and first Eucharist during these primary years.

Intermediate grade students are in a transition period; they may at times seem to be discarding childish behavior but then quickly revert to less appropriate actions. They can be sensitive and moody, and they are beginning to develop their own attitudes and values. These children are strongly motivated by friendly competition, model building, and teamwork and are often drawn to heroes and heroines. They are developing a moral sense and conscience as guides to right behavior.

Intermediate grade students have longer attention spans, a greater facility with reading, and an increased memory for details. Their curriculum examines the guides for Christian living such as the Beatitudes, the Great Commandment, and the Ten Commandments. Students become familiar with biblical heroes, with saints, and with modern day witnesses who put their faith into action and serve as role models. Students study the sacraments in depth and delve into many of the Old Testament Scripture stories.

Early adolescence can be a time of rapid growth on many levels—physical, mental, and emotional. Typically girls mature a bit faster than boys do. Peers become increasingly important, and close friendships develop. A favorite response is "Why?" as these young people seem to question everything. Early adolescents need to be assured of the love of their parents and families, even if they don't openly respond to that love. They can handle abstract concepts and have a sense of history and of social justice.

Catechists can capitalize on this period by continuing to orient their students to deep friendship with Christ, by helping them learn how to witness to Christ, and by showing them how to live, love, and act as Christians. Students become familiar with the Jesus of the Gospels, with the early Church, and with the Church in the world today. An in-depth study of the Creed summarizes the beliefs of the faith. The curriculum also stresses the role of the Church in evangelizing the world and spreading the Gospel through personal witness and action.

Planning Lessons

While the catechist manual provides a well-developed lesson plan for each session, it is unlikely that you will use the plan exactly as is. You need to be flexible and adapt the lessons for the time frame within which you teach; the abilities and learning needs of the students; your own gifts, abilities, and teaching styles; the physical space where you teach; and cultural considerations. Preparing a detailed lesson plan does not stifle the spirit or squelch creativity. It provides a way of organizing your lessons and allows the flexibility to respond to the unexpected promptings of the Holy Spirit and the immediate needs of your students. An effective way to plan lessons is to use a three-step approach that includes: 1) long range planning; 2) short range planning; and 3) writing the actual lesson plan.

Long-range Planning

Begin long range planning with your catechist manual and with a schedule of classes to determine how many sessions you will teach this year. For example, if the Christmas pageant is scheduled on a class day, you may not teach a lesson from your book. Once you determine the exact number of sessions, see how many classes are presented in the textbook. Some textbook sessions may need to be eliminated or combined. If there is a question about which sessions to eliminate, ask your parish director. Next, plan when you will teach seasonal lessons such as in Advent or Lent. Some series place these sessions at the end of the text, so notice where they are located. Mark the dates and topics for the lessons on your class schedule.

Short-range Planning

Several weeks before you teach a lesson, read it over. Study the catechist background information. Think about methods and activities you will use to communicate the message. Request audio-visuals, and purchase or request supplies. Begin to prepare materials for activities. If you are working on a project and need assistance from parents, secure their help early.

This kind of short-range planning allows you to take care of many details ahead of time and will relieve stress when you are ready to write and present your lesson plan.

Immediate Preparation:
Writing the Lesson Plan

As you develop the week's lesson plan, use your catechist manual as a guide. Use a lesson-planning sheet (a sample is included at the end of this chapter). When you write your lesson plan, include the goal or theme of the lesson and the objectives—what students will learn in this lesson. It is helpful to make a step-by-step plan and designate a time frame for each step. List any materials or supplies needed.

A strong catechetical lesson includes several components: life experience, faith dimension/doctrinal, reflection/integration, and response. These components can be woven together throughout the lesson.

LIFE EXPERIENCE

Catechesis addresses learners in the context of their daily lives, so most catechetical lessons begin with the experience of the students. Determine how you will tap into the experiences of the students and initiate their thinking about the theme. Some ways to explore the students' experiences are through questions, a story or audio-visual presentation, using pictures or song, or providing direct experience. For example, a second grade lesson on Eucharist might begin with a discussion of Thanksgiving dinner, or a first grade class on creation could begin with a nature walk.

FAITH DIMENSION AND DOCTRINAL COMPONENT

This is the heart of the lesson. Be certain to have a grasp of the essential teachings of the lesson, and list steps you will take to communicate the teachings in a way that students will understand. The catechist manual is helpful here because it presents the message at an age-appropriate level. Some methods to present these components include:

- ○ brief input sessions
- ○ use of story, song, puppets, drama, or art
- ○ proclamation of the Scriptures
- ○ presentation of concepts for memorization
- ○ use of flannel board, charts, posters

If a lesson contains words that students may not understand, be certain to explain terminology. (We have all heard of the seventh grader who thought the epistles were the wives of the Apostles!) Write down and explain new vocabulary, and show older students where to find it in the glossary of their texts.

REFLECTION AND INTEGRATION

This element of catechesis aims at having students internalize the message and integrate it into their own lives. Obviously, internalization does not happen overnight. You may not immediately see the fruits of your labors. Encourage reflection and integration through use of prayer and quiet time, creative writing, guided meditations, projects related to the theme, and group discussions on well-developed questions.

RESPONSE

Catechetical sessions invite learners to respond to the Word of God in their lives, to deepen their relationship with Jesus Christ, and to become more committed disciples. Even young students are able to make an age-appropriate response to these invitations. Methods which foster such responses include service projects that demonstrate lived response to the message, prayer, celebration of the sacraments, formation of resolutions, and faith-sharing in small groups.

Understand How Students Learn: Learning Styles

As you prepare each lesson, keep in mind that each person has a preferred learning style—a way that they learn best.

○ Some students are **visual learners**. They learn best through seeing things like facial expressions, demonstrations, illustrations, audio-visuals, or by watching a puppet show or dramatic presentation. For these students, simply listening to an explanation is not enough.

○ Some students are **auditory learners.** They learn best through lectures, discussions, talking things through, listening to what others say, and music. For these learners, the written information may have little meaning until it is heard.

○ Some students are **tactile or kinesthetic learners**. They learn best through a hands-on approach. They actively explore the world around them and have difficulty sitting still for long periods. These young people like moving, doing, and touching things.

Additional Activities to Respond to Varying Learning Styles

○ **Individual activities** include memorization, creative writing, reading, drawing, and making posters, collages, scrapbooks, mobiles, dioramas, or using modeling clay.

○ **Group activities** include committee work, guided Internet search, field trips, service projects, dramatic presentations, puppet shows, games, computer presentations, skits, video-making, choral reading, echo pantomime, and making murals and models.

○ **Activities for exchanging ideas** include large group discussions, small group discussions, panel discussions, debates, role playing, open-ended stories, brainstorming, questions and answers, and interviews.

When planning lessons, remember the ways different students learn, and integrate a variety of activities to respond to their differing learning needs. To present dynamic classes in which students enjoy participating, choose several different techniques to uncover the experience of your learners, to reinforce the faith dimension and doctrine, to encourage integration, and to elicit response.

Completing the Lesson Plan Outline

When you complete your lesson plan, write down the major points on 3x5 index cards. Review the points so that you are able to move around the class and are not "glued" to the book. After teaching the lesson, write down what techniques worked well, which activities elicited a favorable response, and which did not seem to work well. A lesson plan for this type of a catechetical session demands several hours of preparation each week. Once you prepare some lessons, planning will become easier, though still time-consuming. After teaching a few sessions, you and your students will develop a rapport, and you will know those activities to which this particular class responds well. With prayer and preparation, you will be well on the way to guiding your students on their extraordinary journey of faith.

Lesson Plan Outline

Date _____

Grade _____

Student Textbook Pages _____

Theme _____

Objectives _____

New Vocabulary _____

Opening Prayer:

Time _____

_____

_____

_____

_____

Life Experience—I will introduce the topic by:

Time _____

1. _____

2. _____

3. _____

Faith Dimension/Doctrinal Component—I will teach this lesson with the following activities, methods, and techniques:

Time _____

1. _____

2. _____

3. _____

4. _____

5. _____

Integration/Reflection—I will encourage integration of the message by:

Time _____

1. _____
2. _____

Response—I will elicit response by:

Time _____

1. _____
2. _____

Comments:

_____
_____
_____
_____
_____
_____
_____
_____
_____

Materials and Supplies Needed:

_____
_____
_____
_____
_____
_____

4

NUTS AND BOLTS

This chapter presents suggestions to help you develop an effective classroom presence, discover how to be an exciting catechist, and manage your class with grace and reassurance.

Know Parish Guidelines

Parish guidelines are developed from experiences in your particular parish. The guidelines are usually discussed at an initial meeting; if you need clarification be sure to ask.

❍ Be especially aware of all guidelines for taking attendance, handling emergency procedures, and implementing safety and evacuation measures.
❍ Know the process if you will be absent.
❍ Follow parish guidelines for discipline.
❍ Know how to request and obtain supplies and whether you will be reimbursed for purchases you make.
❍ If your room is shared with a day-school teacher, respect the classroom setup and the personal property of the teacher and students. If possible, speak with the teacher to determine what you both can do to facilitate the shared use of space.

Develop a Relationship With Your Students

It is important for you to know your young people and their backgrounds. Encourage a communal atmosphere that feels more church-like than school-like. Establish a hospitable setting where children feel comfortable and welcome.

○ Call young people by name. Use nametags or place cards each week until you know everyone by name. Make sure your class knows your name, as well. Some children go through a whole year and cannot name their catechist! Post your name every week at the beginning of the year.

○ Greet students by name as they arrive; plan activities for them to do until class begins.

○ Take a picture of each student on the first day of class. Invite students to write a brief biography on a card, and make a class poster—they like to see themselves!

○ Ask parents to write a letter introducing their child, along with the child's likes, dislikes, hobbies, talents, and family background.

○ Send your students birthday cards or a "we missed you" card when they are absent. Young people love to receive mail! A note from you before sessions even begin will endear you to the students before they ever meet you.

○ Occasionally, call parents with good news reports. Parents enjoy hearing that their children have had an especially great day, and young people will be happy to know that you caught them doing something good!

Create an Environment for Catechesis

Each catechetical session should be conducted in a welcoming, prayerful environment where faith can be experienced and shared. Only God gives the gift of faith, but you can foster an environment where faith can take root, be nourished, grow, and bear fruit.

○ Designate an area of the room as a prayer space where the class gathers for prayer and celebration.

○ Pray with a variety of prayer forms such as group prayer, quiet personal prayer, spontaneous prayer, and guided meditation.

○ Use good liturgical music. Have instrumental music playing as young people arrive. Use music from your parish hymnal for prayer services. If you are not able to sing well, use a CD.

○ Encourage discussion of important points using probing questions that require thought. Allow time for thinking, and then use a quiet voice to encourage student response.

○ Be willing to sidetrack your planned lesson if there is a community concern that affects the lives of your students—they may need to talk about it and pray about it with a caring adult.

Make the Room Your Own

Even if you only use the room once each week, it is important for children to feel that it is *their* space, at least for the hour or so that you are together. This means you will engage in the important ministry of "lugging." Keep it simple, but bring some things each week that let the students know that you have prepared a space for them.

○ Use a cardboard storage box to create an altar. In the box, keep a colored cloth that covers the box (use the appropriate liturgical color), a Bible, votive lights with battery-operated candles (for safety reasons), and a small crucifix. Occasionally, use fresh flowers or a statue of Mary or one of the saints. Ask different children to set up the altar each week. Periodically, ask children to offer a written prayer or artwork to the Lord by placing it around the altar.

○ Make your own portable bulletin board. Purchase a trifold board (used for science project backgrounds) at a craft store. Decorate it and use it to hang a banner announcing the lesson theme, to post prayer responses, or to place a Scripture verse for memorization.

○ Bring a box of supplies if the parish does not provide one. Plastic boxes with handles make excellent supply boxes. Include common office supplies, a note pad, and a flashlight. This will prevent needless trips to the office (or inappropriately going into the desk of the day-school teacher) every time you need an item.

Manage Your Class

Young people need to understand that you are in control of the class. This does not mean that you have to be strict or overly structured, or that children must sit in rows and raise their hands before they can speak. It does mean that you are prepared, organized, and maintain order in a well-disciplined setting. Remember the root of the word "discipline" is *disciple*, meaning "to learn." You want your class of disciples to learn how to follow Jesus, how to conduct themselves in an orderly fashion, and how to respect others and their property. Everyone should know that there are some behaviors that will not be tolerated, and that there are consequences for inappropriate behavior.

○ Set the ground rules in the first or second class. Briefly discuss why rules are important. Guide the young people in creating a set of class rules and stating the rules in a positive, rather than a negative, manner. For example: "Listen quietly when others are speaking"; "Respect others and their property"; "Keep your hands to yourself." Post the rules.

○ Use a variety of methods to teach the same lesson. Elementary students have short attention spans and are more likely to act out if they lose interest. Catechetical sessions are often taught after young people have been in school all day or in the evenings when children are tired. So make your sessions interesting. Do not aim to entertain, but rather to engage and involve students.

○ Do not overreact when a child misbehaves. Some children crave attention and will do anything to draw attention to themselves. When you are disappointed in a behavior, say so. Avoid disciplinary measures that involve name-calling, arguments, confrontation, humiliation, and embarrassment. Never use corporal punishment.

○ Encourage good behavior by using positive reinforcements such as stickers, certificates for great attendance, inviting a student to be a prayer leader or singer, or through affirming statements such as, "Thank you for walking quietly to the prayer area." If you use food treats, make sure they are healthy snacks and that no one has allergies.

○ If a student has a learning disability, ask the parents what accommodations are made for the student in the regular school setting. Try to accommodate the student in a similar way.

○ For some children who consistently present behavior problems, it may be necessary to request a parent conference and to work with the student to develop an individual behavior contract.

Be a Collector

Set aside some space at home to store the "stuff" you will collect. Ask parents, friends, and parishioners to be collectors for you as well.

○ Make a picture file. Scour calendars, travel guides, and magazines for pictures of nature, people (young/old, rich/poor, suffering, helping others), animals, and scenery. Glue pictures on construction paper. Post pictures when you teach about the beauty of creation. Use pictures as an icebreaker with older students—have them select and share a picture that reflects their feelings about the world, the class, the Church, life. Let students match pictures with lines of a psalm or the Stations of the Cross.

○ Collect various containers. Let your imagination run wild. Liquid dish soap containers make great puppets, and when "dressed," can become saints or characters from Scripture. Dress them in felt vestments of appropriate liturgical colors to demonstrate what the priest wears at Mass. Yogurt cups make great planters in which to plant seeds when you talk about the Parable of the Sower or when you teach about death and new life. Cylindrical potato chip holders make great Easter candles when they are covered in white paper, decorated, and "lit" with an orange paper flame.

○ Cardboard from the fronts and backs of cereal boxes makes sturdy backing for puzzles. To make a simple puzzle, use rubber cement and glue a picture from a used religion book. Cut medium size jigsaw puzzle pieces and place in a plastic bag. Have these puzzles available for students who arrive early. Cardboard also makes great patterns for tracing—it is easy to cut and sturdy enough for use by many hands.

Look With the Eyes of a Catechist

Develop a perspective in which you consider how to use seemingly secular activities, projects, games, and crafts to reinforce your catechetical lessons.

○ Adapt seasonal or holiday crafts for your religion lessons. For example, use a simple Valentine's Day heart project to affirm God's love anytime of year.
○ Many newspapers, magazines, and Web sites contain ideas for cards, bookmarks, and small presents. Give these projects scriptural or religious themes, and have students give them as gifts that eucharistic ministers can bring to the homebound parishioners.
○ Keep a scrapbook of project ideas or file them according to theme.

Be a Storyteller

Almost everyone can relate to a good story that captures a slice of life, surfaces dreams or fears, or tells of good overcoming evil. Stories are a great way to surface the experience of your students. Remember, Jesus was a storyteller, so do not hesitate to include some of his stories.

○ Keep a file of stories that tell good news, especially about young people the age of your students—young people serving others, helping family or neighbors, and making good choices. Find stories in the newspaper, magazines, or on the Internet.

○ Practice the story a few times to make sure you have all the elements. If necessary, write it in outline form.

○ Delivery is important. Vary tone of voice, speed of speaking, and facial expression. Use pictures or props to enhance your delivery. For example, one catechist who tells the story of the Good Shepherd to second graders dresses in a tunic, uses a staff, and has several children wear lamb masks.

Use Technology

In this age of technology, our students are greatly influenced by television, music, the Internet, and instant communication. We are challenged and encouraged to use media in our catechesis. "Well-planned catechesis must employ these media so that the message of Jesus Christ can be effectively communicated in the real circumstances and culture of those who seek him" (*NDC* 287). Here are some technology resources to consider:

○ The **Web or Internet** can be a tremendous source of information for catechists. You can find Scripture, Church documents, lives of saints, and theological treatises. However, you need to be aware that not every Web site that claims to be Catholic encompasses the teachings of the Church. If you direct students to a Web site, advise parents, and ask them to assist their children. Catechists should seek information from authentic Catholic sources such as the following:

* The Vatican Web site (www.vatican.va) includes the texts of the documents of the Second Vatican Council, encyclicals and letters of recent popes, virtual tours of Vatican sites, choir music that can be downloaded to MP3 players, a papal calendar, and general information.
* The United States Conference of Catholic Bishops Web site (www.usccb.org) includes a news section, a podcast of daily Scripture readings, ratings for current movies, new releases of DVDs and videos, the entire Bible, and the entire *Catechism of the Catholic Church.*
* Your own diocesan Web site may include diocesan policies and guidelines, recommended textbooks, upcoming classes and workshops, liturgical information, and links to other Catholic Web sites.

○ Web sites for your catechetical textbook series as well as other recommended publishers for your diocese may offer suggestions for catechists, seasonal ideas, and celebrations to all visitors to the site, even if you are not using their textbook.

○ Web sites of Catholic publishers may offer resources. For example, the publisher of this book, Liguori Publications (www.liguori.org), has a Web site that includes publications, a daily reflection, and a place to submit prayer requests. St. Anthony Messenger Press (www.americancatholic.org) includes seasonal inspiration, *Catholic Updates* that can be read online, and a "Saint of the Day" feature. Ask your parish director for the additional names of Catholic publishers and do a "Google" search to visit their Web sites.

○ From time to time, use a short DVD or video in your session to introduce a theme or to summarize a unit. Many parishes and dioceses have media libraries. Some media will provide background information on a theological topic for the catechist; others offer materials for students on sacraments, Scripture stories, prayer, meditations, or moral dilemmas. Always preview materials before you use them with your students, and always have all equipment in working order before starting class.

○ Be aware of the television programs and movies your students are watching. Occasionally use a recap of a current TV program to introduce a topic, or use a TV scene to discuss appropriate or inappropriate behavior.

The next chapters in this handbook include cover topics that are more theological in nature, such as Revelation, Scripture, Church, and the sacraments. These chapters provide valuable background information for you. At the end of each chapter is a section called "Practical Helps for the Catechist" that suggests some creative ways to integrate the chapter themes into your lessons.

5

REVELATION, SCRIPTURE AND TRADITION

Our God is an awesome God worthy of praise, honor, and reverence! Our God loves us with unconditional love, creates us in his own image, and accompanies us with his unending presence. Throughout the history of our salvation, God has chosen to be a revealing God, a communicating God, a self-disclosing God. This self-revelation of God is pure gift and grace, given to us at God's own initiative.

Imagine a magnificent game of divine hide and seek between God and his people. No matter how often the people hide or turn away, God seeks and finds them and continues to reveal more abundant love, more compassion, more forgiveness, and more healing.

Revelation in the Old Testament

In the garden story (Genesis 3:1–24), Adam and Even hide after they disobey God, but God seeks them out and promises a Messiah and Redeemer (see *CCC* 410). Through Noah, Abraham, and Sarah, Jacob, Joseph, and Moses, the Israelites understand that God wants to reveal himself through saving actions in their lives. God repeatedly seeks out the people of Israel and offers them a covenant relationship: he will be their God, and they will be his people. This covenant is solidified in the Passover and Exodus experiences when God saves the Israelites by the blood of the lamb and leads them to freedom through the Red Sea.

Whenever the Israelites hide from keeping their covenant relationship with God, God seeks them out through Prophets, Judges, and Kings, who call them back to their unique relationship with the God who has never left them. Through God's gradual but continual self-revelation, the Israelites come to a more explicit understanding, a clearer knowledge, and a deeper belief in the one God who calls them out of bondage and into freedom.

The Old Testament reveals God's promise and God's loving plan to save humanity. God's plan is made possible through the faith-filled response of Mary, "...a unique vessel of God's Revelation..." (*NDC* 43). It is Mary's "yes" that allows God to fully reveal himself. It is Mary's response in faith that allows the Word of God to become flesh.

The Fullness of God's Revelation

The summit of God's self-communication is found in the person of Jesus Christ. He is the ultimate Word spoken by God, the culmination of God's revelation. The Gospel of John notes "In the beginning...the Word was with God, and the Word was God....[a]nd the Word became flesh..." (1:1–14). God spoke everything that needed to be said when the Word became flesh in the Incarnation. There is nothing to be revealed about God—about God's mercy, God's love, God's fidelity, God's forgiveness, God's justice, etc.—that has not already been revealed in Jesus Christ, "...the image of the invisible God" (Colossians 1:15). No new public revelation will be given until the end of time when Christ comes in glory. "The process of Revelation, which took centuries to unfold, reached its magnificent fulfillment in the life, death, and Resurrection of Jesus Christ" (*USCCA* 13).

Some people may experience personal manifestations of God's love, mercy, or healing or see God manifested in the beauty of creation. There are private revelations, such as apparitions at Fatima. But neither personal manifestations nor private revelations add anything "...to what was publicly revealed up and through Christ..." (*USCCA* 15).

It is through Jesus Christ that the central mystery of the Trinity is revealed. Through Jesus, we come to know three divine persons in one God—the Father, the Son, and the Holy Spirit. These divine persons, distinct yet inseparable, are revealed in who they are and what they do: the Father through the work of creating, the Son through the work of redeeming, and the Holy Spirit through the work of sanctifying.

God's Revelation Requires a Response

In the same way that God's self-communication called for a response from our ancestors in faith, God's revelation calls for a response today. We respond to God's revelation in faith, in belief, in conversion, and in gratitude. It is faith that turns us to God, to trust when times are dark or difficult, and to believe even when God seems absent. It is in faith that we understand the God who is not hidden but actively seeks us. It is in faith that we embrace the teachings handed down through the ages. It is in faith that we continue to see God through the person of Jesus Christ.

As a catechist, you want to present the loving triune God to young people in a way that will empower them to know God, to love God, and to serve God. You want to ignite in young people a yearning for the God in whose image they were formed—the God who desires that they are fully human and fully alive. You want to help them seek God who loves them, who knows them by name, and who walks with them every day. You want to encourage them to find the God who is not hidden but who actively seeks them.

Sacred Scripture

God's revelation is preserved and handed down in the Church through Scripture and Tradition. The sacred Scriptures, contained in the Bible, are a principal source of catechesis.

The Bible is comprised of forty-six books of the Old Testament and twenty-seven books of the New Testament, which together reveal God's loving plan of salvation.

As Catholics, we understand that the Scriptures are the Word of God, written by human authors who were inspired and guided by the Holy Spirit. These Scriptures contain the "...truths necessary for our salvation," and are "...truly the Word and work of God" (*USCCA* 27). The Scriptures reflect God's saving actions in history and give meaning to historical events, but do not necessarily present absolute historical facts. The Scriptures do not give us history as we know it today.

The Bible is a collection of books—a library of divinely inspired books containing different types of literature. To understand the Scriptures more completely, it is necessary to be aware of the literary style and form that each author used. Some of the books are inspired history (such as Exodus), inspired poetry (such as Psalms), inspired prophecy (such as

Isaiah), inspired satire (such as Jonah), inspired parable (such as Job), inspired correspondence (such as Corinthians), or inspired Gospel (such as Matthew). If we fail to understand the type of literature that the human author used, the truth that the author intended to convey can be masked or missed.

Readers of the Scriptures should also understand that the stories and events that reveal God's love and saving plan were first handed down by word of mouth from generation to generation. Over more than eleven centuries, parts of this oral tradition were merged, integrated, and written down. The "Canon of Scripture"—the term used to describe the seventy-three books of the Bible that the Church understands as divinely inspired—was agreed on during the first centuries of the Church.

The Old Testament

The Old Testament contains many different literary forms and styles. The Law or *Torah* is contained in the first five books. These books, revered by the Jewish people, tell the story of how God formed the Israelites as a people, and lay out laws and commandments that help the Israelites fulfill the covenant. The Old Testament also includes history, poetry, fable, genealogies, and prophecies. Many of the songs found in the Psalms give praise to God; others offer consolation and encouragement to those who pray and sing them. Some of the most beautiful writings are found in the Prophets, such as those of Isaiah or Hosea, who invite people to return to the intimate relationship that God desires. From the Christian stance, the Old Testament Law, prophecies, and covenant find fulfillment and completion in Jesus Christ.

The New Testament

The New Testament is a collection of literary works written by various authors to varying audiences:

The Gospels or Good News are a literary form that is unique to Christianity. These four books are central in the life of the Church because at the center of the Gospels we find Jesus. Written approximately forty to seventy years after the resurrection of Christ, they were meant for particular communities with particular needs. The Gospel writers brought their own personalities and experiences to their writing. They chose stories, narratives, and sayings of Jesus that they thought would be helpful to their communities.

While the authors of the Gospels are not named in the texts, the Church called them Matthew, Mark, Luke (the Synoptic Gospels, because they are very similar), and John. All of the Gospels are written through the lens of Easter faith, proclaiming that Jesus is alive and risen from the dead. While there were many other Gospels written in the early history of Christianity, the Church preserved these four Gospels as faithfully expressing the life and teaching of Jesus Christ and the preaching of the Apostles.

The **epistles** are twenty-one letters written by Paul, James, Peter, and others whose names are unknown. Most of these letters, which give encouragement, exhortation, and guidance to members of the fledgling Christian community, were written before the Gospels.

The **Acts of the Apostles** gives a glimpse of early church community and its structures. It demonstrates how the Apostles and disciples preached, taught, and spread the message about Jesus Christ.

The **Book of Revelation** uses symbolic language to bring hope and encouragement to the early church as it underwent persecution.

Tradition

Jesus commissioned the Apostles to teach and to preach the Gospel. Once the Apostles received the gift of the Holy Spirit, they went out and boldly proclaimed the message of Christ by preaching about the resurrected Lord. From the beginning, successors to the Apostles were chosen as bishops to continue the mission and ministry of Christ and to conserve the authentic teaching of the Church. In every age, through this apostolic succession, the Church hands on and interprets the Word of God as it is found in Scripture and Tradition, which together comprise the Deposit of Faith. "The Church performs this function authoritatively through her living, teaching office, the Magisterium. The Magisterium insures the Church's fidelity to the teaching of the apostles in matters of faith and morals" (*NDC* 53–54).

As a catechist, you know that God has revealed himself through Scripture and the living Tradition of the Church. A study of Scripture and Church teachings will deepen your own understanding and help you uncover the awesome God who continues to seek and to find us.

PRACTICAL HELPS FOR THE CATECHIST

Use a variety of resources to help your students know and learn about God who reveals himself in Scripture and Tradition:

○ Each week enthrone the Bible by opening it and reverently placing it on your classroom altar as you begin class.

○ Every time you use the Bible for prayer, be sure to proclaim the reading directly from the Bible. If you or a student reads from the Bible, show reverence for the Word of God by gently bowing before the open Bible.

○ Have groups of older students create their own videos by retelling one of the parables using a current life situation.

○ Read a Scripture passage and have students pantomime as you read, or use flannel boards or puppets to depict a story.

○ Let students create a group mural of an event that happens over time, such as the Exodus, or of a parable with several parts, such as the Prodigal Son.

○ Use pictures from your picture file or computer images of photos to pray the Psalms.

○ Teach older students how to look up references in the Bible. Then conduct a relay where students take turns looking up a list of biblical references that you have prepared. Students look up the passage, write down the person or item mentioned, and then pass the Bible and list to the next student. For example, if one reference is Matthew 16:16, the appropriate answer is Simon Peter. This activity helps students to locate book, chapter, and verse.

○ Begin and end class with the Sign of the Cross, the trinitarian prayer that recalls our baptism in the name of Father, Son, and Holy Spirit.

6

JESUS CHRIST: TRUE GOD AND TRUE MAN

In 1934, Harry Warren and Al Dubin composed a beautiful love song entitled "I Only Have Eyes for You." The song has had sustained appeal through the decades with renditions by Frank Sinatra, the Lettermen, and even a male penguin in the movie, *Happy Feet*. The lyrics immortalize lovers whose love blinds them to the stars, clouds, gardens, and people who pass by—all they can see is each other. When two people are in love, they spend quality time learning about each other, discovering each other's likes and dislikes, personalities, deepest longings, and future wishes. If they decide to marry, they enjoy meeting family members and learning of the background of their future spouse. They delight in listening to stories about their intended and in looking at photos and videos from earlier years. They want to know all about this person with whom they will enter an intimate and lifelong union.

In the same way, you will want to know all about Jesus the Christ who is the center and focus of all catechesis. You will want to scour the Scriptures for glimpses of what Jesus said and did while he walked the earth. You will be interested to see how the early Church responded to the life, death, and resurrection of Jesus, and you will look to Church Tradition to see how the Church's understanding of Jesus Christ (its Christology) developed and was passed on through generations. You will try to learn as much as you can about Jesus Christ, who loves you with an everlasting love. You will strive to deepen your own intimate relationship with Christ, true God and true man, and second person of the Trinity. You will encourage your students to have this same kind of curiosity about Jesus so that their relationship with him can grow, deepen, and mature.

Who Do You Say That I Am?

More than 2000 years ago, Jesus asked Peter, "Who do you say that I am?" (Matthew 16:15). Today Jesus asks for a response to this same question. Your response to Jesus' question may have changed throughout the years—one response when you were a child, another as a teen, and still another today. Your experiences of Jesus, your training, your spirituality, your understanding of the Scriptures, and your maturity in faith ultimately should lead you to make a faith-filled confession similar to Peter's: "You are the Christ," "You are the Lord," "You are the Messiah."

Jesus Christ in the New Testament

One of the first things that the Gospels relate about Jesus is that he was Jewish. He was born into a Jewish family; he participated in Jewish feasts, traditions, and celebrations; he went to the synagogue and the Temple; he was familiar with the Hebrew Scriptures; and he understood the covenant. Jesus often quotes from the Psalms, the Law, and the Prophets, and he makes references to ancestors in faith. Through the eyes of resurrection faith, the Gospel and epistles writers acknowledge Jesus as the perfection of the Law, the realization of Old Testament prophecies, and the fulfillment of the New Covenant.

Only two of the Gospels (Matthew and Luke) recount infancy narratives or stories about Jesus' birth. Differing somewhat in the details that they relate, both accounts disclose the humanity and the divinity of Jesus. The beginning of John's Gospel clearly affirms the divine nature of Jesus, the Word made flesh. The Gospels tell little about Jesus' life until he began preaching and teaching—except when the twelve-year-old Jesus is found teaching in the Temple, which he calls his Father's house.

Jesus spends most of the three years of his public life preaching and teaching about the kingdom of God and how to prepare for its coming. He accomplishes miracles and signs, demonstrating that the kingdom is breaking through and is already present. He tells parables about the mustard seed, hidden treasure, and yeast to teach people what the kingdom of God is like.

The Gospels present a portrait of the human Jesus as an extremely charismatic teacher, preacher, and healer who is deeply moved by the plight of those who are excluded, rejected, or forgotten. Jesus is a man who experiences strong human emotions—he weeps at the death of his friend; is angered at commercial dealings in the Temple; is frustrated with disciples who misunderstand his teaching; and is grieved at rejection, denial, and betrayal. Jesus experiences real pain and suffering during his scourging and crucifixion.

Throughout his ministry, Jesus reveals God's universal and unconditional love, which is not earned, but freely given to all. Using parables such as the Prodigal Son, the Good Shepherd, and the Lost Sheep, Jesus surprises people as they learn about God's tremendous patience, overwhelming generosity, unending love, and gracious salvation. He has an intimate relationship with God, his Father. Through his actions, Jesus shows God's desire to forgive, to heal, to heap mercy, and to bring justice to all people. In hearing Jesus, people hear the voice of God. In seeing Jesus, they see the face of God.

Jesus considers suffering and the cross essential parts of his mission. On several occasions, he predicts his suffering and death, and he willingly journeys to Jerusalem in spite of the protests of his disciples. Jesus accepts his Father's will, embraces suffering and death with open arms, and freely offers his life and spirit back to his Father.

The New Testament writers understood that the sacrifice of Jesus brought salvation to humanity. His obedience to the Father's will substituted for the disobedience of the human race (see *CCC* 615). "Our salvation flows from God's initiative of love for us, because 'he loved us and sent his Son to be the expiation for our sins' [1 John 4:10]" (*CCC* 620). In Christ, God reconciled the world to himself (see 2 Corinthians 5:19).

Following his death on the cross, Jesus is buried; on the third day he rises from the dead. The Gospels do not describe the actual resurrection, but they relate the empty tomb, the burial cloths, and the appearances of Jesus to the disciples. The glorious, resurrected body of Christ bears the marks of his suffering and death. But this glorified body is not limited by time and space—it is no longer in the human realm. The Paschal Mystery (the passion, death, and resurrection of Christ) "...has two aspects: by his death, Christ liberates us from sin; by his Resurrection, he opens for us the way to a new life" (*CCC* 654). Christ's sacrifice on the cross has atoned for our sin; Christ's resurrection from the dead provides hope for our own resurrection. "Just as in Adam all die, so in Christ all will come to life again..." (1 Corinthians 15:22). A Memorial Acclamation used in the Liturgy succinctly expresses our belief and hope: "Dying you destroyed our death; rising you restored our life."

Before he ascends, Jesus entrusts his followers with a mission to make disciples, to baptize, and to teach. Then he promises his presence until the end of the world (see Matthew 28:18–20).

Jesus Christ in the Tradition of the Church

The Acts of the Apostles and the Epistles provide an understanding of what the early Church believed about the humanity and divinity of Jesus. They describe Jesus using titles that provide insight into the faith of early Christians:

○ *Christ or Messiah*, which revealed his divine mission (see *CCC* 438)
○ *Son of God*, which showed his divinity
○ *Lord*, which showed that the honor and glory "...due to God the Father [were] due also to Jesus..." (*CCC* 449)

These communities also used brief formulas to express their faith and belief in Jesus, such as "...[I]f you confess with your lips that Jesus is Lord and believe in your heart that God raised him from the dead, you will be saved" (Romans 10:9). Their belief in Jesus as God and man is beautifully expressed in a hymn that tells of Christ who was in the form of God but humbled himself and became man (see Philippians 2). Many of the first disciples were martyred because of their belief in the name and power of Jesus.

During the first few centuries, leaders of the blossoming Church convened several councils in order to clarify Church teachings and beliefs as controversies or heresies arose. For example, the Council of Nicea (325 AD) declared that Jesus Christ was "...the Son of God by nature and not by adoption" and that he was "'begotten' not made" and was "of the same substance as the Father" (*USCCA* 82). The Council of Chalcedon (451 AD) proclaimed that Jesus Christ was true God and true man. The councils often developed professions of faith, or creeds, as symbols of the faith. Catholics are most familiar with the Apostles' Creed, considered to be a summary of the faith of the Apostles, and the Nicene Creed, usually prayed in the Sunday Liturgy and common to the churches of both the East and the West.

Through the centuries, the Church has consistently presented a Christology that asserts that Jesus Christ is true God and true man, that he restored the harmony between God and humanity ruptured by sin, and that his sacrifice brought redemption and salvation for all. Early Church father, Saint Athanasius, stated it beautifully: "For the Son of God became man so that we might become God" (quoted in *CCC* 460).

PRACTICAL HELPS FOR THE CATECHIST

Use of a variety of methods to encourage your students to know Jesus Christ, true God and true man:

○ Allow younger children to act out a Gospel story and put on the "persona" of the various characters. Have a container of fabric for costumes and of props that appear often in stories or parables: fish, nets, coins, seeds, salt, shepherd's staff, etc.

○ Create bumper stickers or doorknob hangers with titles of Jesus that reflect his divinity.

○ Send older students on a New Testament scavenger hunt, scouring the Gospels or epistles for names and titles of Jesus.

○ Let students make and illustrate a booklet of ten important sayings of Jesus. Place them in a time capsule (decorate a round potato chip container) for future generations!

○ Use creative writing—have students answer the question of Jesus to Peter, "Who do you say that I am?"

○ Encourage younger children to learn the Our Father by heart. Use a version put to music and gestures, and ask parents to pray the Our Father with their children.

○ Assist older children to learn the Apostles' Creed and the Nicene Creed, being certain that they understand what each part means.

○ Have older students write articles for the front page of a newspaper whose headline reads: "Jesus Christ Is Risen from the Dead!" Publish your newspaper for the parish at Easter, or perhaps include it as a bulletin insert or "Extra!" that students, as greeters, can hand to parishioners.

7

THE CHURCH

A sk a group of twenty parishioners to describe "Church" and you will undoubtedly receive twenty unique and diverse responses. Their descriptions are likely to be influenced by age, cultural and ethnic background, education, spiritual formation, and involvement in Church life. Some people may describe the building; others may refer to the sense of community they experience; still others may refer to the service that is offered to the poor. Some may understand the Church as an institution; still others may describe Church in terms of the Word that is proclaimed and the sacraments that are celebrated. Some may focus on the Church as a group of disciples on a mission. You may even find a few people who will combine the above descriptions to define Church.

When the Second Vatican Council leaders sought to describe the Church in the *Dogmatic Constitution on the Church,* they used numerous images to express the reality of Church: a sacrament, a sign, an instrument, a sheepfold, a flock, a cultivated field, our mother, the building of God, a bride, a society, a stranger in a foreign land, a pilgrim. The number of images that they used suggests the elusive and ungraspable reality and mystery of the Church.

Council Fathers, after affirming that the Church is a mystery both human and divine, explained the Church most often as the "People of God." All the People of God are called to holiness, and all participate in the saving mission of the Church in a unique way, depending on their call and roles.

The Church Is a Mystery

The Church is a mystery—human and divine, visible and spiritual—that has its origins in the Trinity. "The Father called the Church into existence. The Son established the Church. The Holy Spirit filled the Church with power and wisdom at Pentecost....The Church, empowered by the Holy Spirit, brings Christ's salvation to the world. She is the instrument of God's universal call to holiness" (*USCCA* 112–13). Christ is dynamically present in the Church through his Spirit, whose gifts are lavishly given to encourage, inspire, and build up the People of God so that they are empowered to serve. The redeeming work of Christ continues in the Church through preaching of the Word, celebrating the sacraments, and serving those in need.

Christ gave his followers a mission to evangelize—to go out and make disciples of all nations. This evangelizing mission of the Church continues when men and women enthusiastically spread the "good news" about Jesus Christ.

The Marks of the Church

There are several defining characteristics or marks that identify the Church. At Sunday Mass, we pray and affirm these marks in the Nicene Creed: the Church is one, holy, catholic, and apostolic.

○ The Church is **one** and confesses one baptism, one faith, one Lord, and one Body of Christ. This unity comes from Christ and not from the Church's own power. The *Catechism* is clear in this regard when it states: "The Church is one because of her source...The Church is one because of her founder...The Church is one because of her soul: It is the Holy Spirit, dwelling in those who believe...who brings about that wonderful communion of the faithful" (*CCC* 813). Sadly, in the history of the Church, there have been schisms and divisions. But the Church actively seeks reconciliation with separated brothers and sisters through ecumenical dialogue.

○ The Church is **holy** because it originates with the Trinity. Holiness is the vocation and call of all its members. Mary and the saints are models and witnesses who have responded to the call.

○ The Church is **catholic** or universal. Missionary in nature and reaching out to bring the Gospel to all people, the Church proclaims the fullness of faith and invites response to the faith. This worldwide Church seeks to root the Gospel message into the culture of the people. Through the "dynamic process" of inculturation, the Church listens "...to the culture of the people for an echo of the word of God," and the Church discerns "...openness to authentic Gospel values in the culture" (*NDC* 64). When necessary, the Church identifies "...elements in the culture that may be hostile or adverse to the Gospel" (*NDC* 64) and then invites conversion to the Gospel message.

○ The Church is **apostolic**. It is built on the lasting foundation of the Apostles. Christ teaches, serves, and sanctifies through the pope and the bishops of the world, who are the successors of Peter and the Apostles.

Roles and Ministries in the Church

The word "church" comes from a Greek word *ekklesia*, which means "convocation" or "gathering of people." The Church is a gathering of the baptized who, by virtue of their baptism, share in the mission and ministry of Christ. Within the Church, there are specific structures and roles.

○ The **pope**, successor to Saint Peter, is the visible head of the Church and has full power in the Church (see *USCCA* 523). Through the gift of infallibility, which the Holy Spirit gives to the Church, "...the pope, and bishops in communion with him—can definitively proclaim a doctrine of faith and morals, which is divinely revealed for the belief of the faithful" (*USCCA* 516).

○ The **bishops**, successors to the Apostles, teach and conserve the faith. Bishops exercise their pastoral duties over a diocese, which is usually comprised of many parishes. "Their authority must be exercised in communion with the whole Church under the guidance of the Pope" (*CCC* 895).

○ **Priests** are ordained by a bishop and are most often responsible for teaching, guiding, preaching, and celebrating the sacraments in their parishes. Coworkers to their bishops, priests are responsible for shepherding God's people and encouraging the participation in the evangelizing mission of the Church.

○ **Deacons** are ordained by a bishop and dedicated to works of charity. They may baptize, proclaim the Gospel, preach the homily, bless marriages, and preside at funerals (see *USCCA* 509).

○ **Laypeople** (those who are not ordained) share in the priesthood of Christ by virtue of their baptism. While many laypeople are involved in parish ministries, they also have an essential and more pressing role in carrying out the mission of the Church. They bring the Church's mission into the context of their daily lives—their families, their neighborhoods, their social lives, and their workplaces—by bringing the love and message of Christ to these environments. Laypeople give witness to Christ by living lives based on Christ's teaching and values, by serving the poor, and by working to change unjust social structures. Laypeople "… are in the unique position of being able directly to infuse culture and society with the Gospel" (*USCCA* 134).

○ Additionally, some laypeople are recognized as being gifted for ministry within the Church. These ministers, named lay **ecclesial ministers**, are prepared theologically and formed spiritually, and are credentialed by their dioceses. This ministry does not take the place of ordained ministry, but is complimentary to it. It includes ministries such as those of pastoral associate, catechetical leader, youth minister, and liturgical minister.

○ There are also, within the Church, women and men who witness to Christ by living a consecrated life in community and by taking the vows of poverty, chastity, and obedience. Many of these **priests, brothers, and women religious** are involved in the teaching and serving ministries in the Church.

Mary, Mother of God
and Mother of the Church

The Church consistently looks to Mary, Mother of Christ and Mother of the Church, for guidance, inspiration, and protection. "Mary's role in the Church is inseparable from her union with Christ and flows directly from it" (*CCC* 964). Mary is honored with many titles and is revered as patroness of the United States under the title "Immaculate Conception" and as the patroness of the Americas under the title "Our Lady of Guadalupe."

Mary is an example for the Church and for all believers because she was completely open to the will of God, to the redeeming work of his Son, and to the promptings of the Holy Spirit (see *CCC* 967). She is a model of discipleship for all believers. Mary's unconditional "yes" gives birth to Christ in the world. Her deep faith in his power calls forth his ministry at Cana. Her love and fidelity call her to the foot of his cross. Her hope places her in the upper room awaiting the gift of the Spirit.

In 1854, Pope Pius IX infallibly declared the Dogma of the Immaculate Conception—that Mary was conceived without original sin. In 1950, Pope Pius XII infallibly declared the Dogma of the Assumption—that following her earthly life, Mary was assumed into heaven, body and soul.

The Saints:
Witnesses to Living a Christian Life

Within our history as a Church, there have always been holy men and women who have shown us how to follow and imitate Christ. By living lives in communion with the Trinity, these saints demonstrate how we can be open to God's goodness, grace, and action in our own lives. Through their witness, we understand how to live lives based on Gospel values. Through a process called canonization, the Church has solemnly declared that these men and women should be venerated as saints.

Meditating on the lives of the saints and reading their writings can inspire us and deepen our spirituality. In responding to God's call, many of these saints underwent dramatic conversions after living very colorful lives. Many embraced physical deprivations and hardships, mental and spiritual anguish, and even martyrdom as they witnessed to Christ.

PRACTICAL HELPS FOR THE CATECHIST

Use a variety of activities to acquaint your young people with the many facets of Church:

○ Arrange for a tour of the church building so that your students are familiar with the physical characteristics of the church. Or take photos and present a PowerPoint presentation.
○ Visit the pastor in his office (or the rectory, if he is willing). Many young people do not know the pastor or what he does. Ask him to give a brief talk to older students about the work of the parish.
○ Have your young people work with adults in parish service projects; even young children can sort food or collect items like socks or mittens.
○ Divide older students into groups of three or four. Let students read through articles or stories on individual saints and develop and perform skits. Present the skits to other students around All Saints Day.

○ Make sure younger children know the Hail Mary. Older students should be familiar with the mysteries of the rosary and how to pray the rosary.
○ Ask parents to assist their children in visiting the Vatican Web site (www.vatican.va) and taking a virtual tour of the Sistine Chapel. This exciting Web site will give young people a sense of the catholic/universal Church.

8

PRAYER AND LITURGY

The night before Benjamin's eighth birthday, his mom over-
heard his prayer. "Hi God, it's me, Benjamin. Please give
me a bicycle for my birthday." Mom was concerned—a bike
was not among the presents. After the gifts were opened, they
had a chance to chat. Mom said, "Ben, I'm sorry God didn't
answer your prayer." Ben's faith-filled reply: "Oh, Mom, God
did answer my prayer. God said 'No.'" Ben's response reveals
his healthy relationship with God. Ben speaks with God and
expects an answer. Perhaps it's not the answer Ben had hoped
for, but it is an answer nonetheless.

Prayer Is Communicating With God

Prayer is very personal—it is raising our hearts and minds to
God, communicating with God, and deepening our relationship
with God. The starting point of all prayer is an awareness of
the presence of the God who is always with us. Our *life* should
be a prayer: all our works and words, our joys and sorrows, all
that we do each day, should be directed toward God. Prayer
is speaking and listening to our God, who responds sometimes in words, sometimes in actions or experiences, often

in surprises. As with any relationship, prayer takes time and intentionality.

In the Gospels, Jesus often leaves the hustle and bustle of his ministry and makes time to pray. He also teaches us how to pray by beseeching God our Father. Jesus prays in the garden and as he dies. After Jesus' ascension, the disciples devote themselves to constant prayer as they await the gift of the Spirit. "The infant Church was born in prayer, lived in prayer, and thrived in prayer" (*USCCA* 467). Paul tells us to pray all the time (1 Thessalonians 5:17). Through the centuries, holy men and women have devoted themselves to lives of prayer, spiritual reading, and writing.

Prayer involves speaking, but it also includes listening—it is essential to have quiet time to be still and listen. Developing our relationship with God entails seeing how God has acted in the past. It is important to read the Scriptures and spiritual books during our prayer time. Furthering our relationship with God means being in community with those who are also in relationship with God. It is crucial to pray as a community.

Forms and Purposes of Prayer

There are many types of prayer. Our prayer can be traditional or formal—for example, the Our Father, the Nicene Creed, the Act of Contrition, grace before meals. Or we can pray in a more informal style using our own words. We can pray spontaneously whenever we choose, and we can pray as a community at Mass, at the celebration of the sacraments, and in small groups. We can verbalize our prayer, meditate in silence, and contemplate in stillness. We can sing, dance, or gesture our prayer; we may stand, sit, lie prostrate, kneel, genuflect, or bow in prayer. The possibilities for prayer are as numerous as those who pray!

There are many reasons to pray, and the acronym ACTS assists us in remembering these purposes: Adoration, Contrition, Thanksgiving, and Supplication.

○ **Adoration and Praise**: We pray to adore and to praise God, who is all-present, all-powerful, and worthy of all honor and glory. We adore and praise God simply because God is God, and we are his creatures

○ **Contrition**: We pray in a spirit that asks for forgiveness and expresses sorrow for our sins. In humility we pray to God who is merciful, life-giving, and compassionate. We ask for the strength to live more fully according to God's purposes.

○ **Thanksgiving**: We pray to thank God for the sum total of our lives, all that we are and all that we have. We are thankful even for painful times, which God can use to draw us closer to him. Our most beautiful prayer of thanksgiving is our active participation in the Eucharist.

○ **Supplication or Petition**: We pray for our needs and for the needs of others, acknowledging our total dependence on God. We are aware that God knows our deepest needs and desires even before we ask, and we trust that God answers our prayer according to his will.

Liturgy, the Prayer of the Church

The word *liturgy* comes from a Greek word that means *work of the people*. Liturgy is the work of the entire Church and encompasses all the rites and rituals through which the Church publicly worships the triune God. It includes the Mass; the sacraments; rites such as Christian burial; the blessing of holy water, palms, and ashes; and the Liturgy of the Hours. The Liturgy of the Hours (or Divine Office) is a prayer of the Church that includes Scripture, psalms, canticles, and intercessions. It is prayed each day at specific times: morning, mid-morning, midday, mid-afternoon, evening, and bedtime. Praying the Liturgy of the Hours has a cherished history in the Church, and through the centuries, Hours have been prayed by the or-dained and by members of religious orders. Since Vatican II, many parishes have revived this tradition and pray Morning Prayer or Evening Prayer as a community.

Christ is alive and at work in his Church through the eu-charistic liturgy, which is the "source and summit" of power and activity (Dogmatic Constitution on the Church [*Lumen Gentium*], 11). At the Mass, Christ is present in many ways: in the Scripture that is proclaimed, in the people gathered, in the priest who presides, and most especially, in the Eucharist that is celebrated. We respond to Christ's presence in the liturgy with "full, conscious, and active participation" (Constitution on the Sacred Liturgy [*Sacrosanctum Concilium*], 14). It is liturgy that helps to define us as the "People of God."

The Materials of Liturgy

The liturgy uses materials and actions to accomplish its work. In its liturgical rites and rituals, the Church uses the "stuff" of our senses:

○ objects we can see such as candles, oil, wedding rings, ashes, and water
○ actions we can feel such as the touch of hands being laid on those who are sick

○ things we can hear, such as the Word proclaimed, music, and prayers
○ items we can smell, such as incense
○ objects we can taste, such as bread and wine
○ movements such as kneeling, standing, bowing, processing
○ gestures such as the sign of peace
○ colors that reinforce the theme of a feast or season
   ∗ white or gold—joy, honor, praise
   ∗ red—the Holy Spirit, martyrdom
   ∗ violet/purple—waiting, penance, sorrow
   ∗ green—hope

The Liturgical Year

The Church celebrates the life, death, and resurrection of Christ throughout the span of an entire year—a liturgical year that begins on the first Sunday of Advent and concludes with the feast of Christ the King. Within this sacred calendar, every Sunday is kept holy as the Lord's Day—the day that extends Christ's resurrection throughout the entire year.

The liturgical year is divided into seasons, feasts, and ordinary time:

○ **Advent**, the beginning of the new Church year, is a season when a new cycle of readings begins. The Church uses a three-year cycle of Sunday readings: most of the Gospel readings in Year A are from Matthew, in Year B from Mark, and in Year C from Luke. During Advent, we prepare for Christ's coming at the end of time, Christ's coming at Christmas, and Christ's coming each day. Liturgical color: violet or purple.

○ **Christmas Time** extends from Christmas Day until the feast of the Baptism of the Lord in January. We celebrate Christ's Incarnation, the feast of the Holy Family, the solemnity of Mary, and the Epiphany. Liturgical color: white or gold.

○ There are two periods of **Ordinary Time** in each liturgical year—one between Christmas Time and Lent; the other between Easter Time and Advent. Ordinary means normal or standard time in the Church calendar. For more than thirty weeks, Sundays have a dominant character where we learn how to carry out the mission of Christ. Liturgical color: green.

○ **Lent** is celebrated for forty days between Ash Wednesday and the Easter Triduum. It is a time of fasting, penance, almsgiving, and good works in preparation for the resurrection of the Lord. It is also a time of retreat for the elect, those people preparing for initiation at the Easter Vigil. Liturgical color: purple.

○ The **Easter Triduum** is the summit or high point of the liturgical year, lasting from Holy Thursday until Easter Sunday at sundown. Liturgically, these three days are considered one celebration in which the Paschal Mystery unfolds. We celebrate the institution of the Eucharist (liturgical color: white), the commemoration of the suffering and death of Jesus (liturgical color: red), and Christ's resurrection from the dead (liturgical color: white or gold). At the Easter Vigil, the new fire is lit, the *Exsultet* proclaims Christ is risen from the dead, holy water is blessed, and baptismal vows are renewed. The Elect are fully initiated into the Church.

○ Easter Time lasts for fifty glorious days from Easter Sunday until Pentecost. The Church celebrates the resurrection with joyful spirits, alleluias, bells, and wonderful music. Most of the Gospel readings, telling of the post-resurrection appearances of Jesus, are from John. Liturgical color: white.

PRACTICAL HELPS FOR THE CATECHIST

Use a variety of activities to help young people learn more about prayer and liturgy:

❍ Incorporate several prayer forms in your sessions. Include guided meditations, a litany, or a procession. Students should know and pray formal prayers *and* have opportunities to pray spontaneously. Encourage prayers of petition or litanies of thanksgiving.

❍ Plan a structured prayer service to summarize a unit. Invite students to serve as prayer leader, cantor, reader, or musician. Elements of a simple service could include:

✻ Theme—base the theme of the service on the lesson or unit.

✻ Environment—use appropriate liturgical color and a symbol from the lesson – for example, seeds or water.

✻ Song—sing the refrain of a song from your parish hymnal that fits the theme.

✻ Prayer—use a formal prayer, a prayer from your text, or a prayer of praise.

✻ Reading—use a short Scripture reading from the lesson or unit.

✻ Response—pray or sing a short psalm or use a guided meditation on the reading. Ask your parish director for books of guided meditations for children.

✻ Pray—share spontaneous prayers of intercession.

✻ Closing Prayers—pray the Our Father and the Sign of the Cross.

- Assist students in memorizing their prayers by making prayer puzzles. Use your computer and break a lengthy prayer (like the Nicene Creed) into phrases, placing each phrase on a new page. Mix the sheets up and let students work in small groups to put the prayer in order. When all groups are finished, pray the prayer together. Create a smaller version of the puzzles, place them in envelopes, and ask parents to help their children learn the prayer at home.
- Familiarize students with liturgical colors by making vestments out of felt or colored paper. Cut an oval shape of fabric or paper with a small hole in the center. Have students dress puppets with appropriate colors for each Sunday.
- Make procession streamers using plastic tablecloths in liturgical colors. Cut one-inch wide strips and staple them to paper tubes.
- Bring older students to the sacristy of your church. Ask one of the priests or liturgical ministers to demonstrate the vestments, the altar linens, the sacred vessels, and other items used for Liturgy.
- Ask parents to help students make altar dioramas using shoeboxes. Suggest the use of small items from around the house; altar furnishings could be made from wood, clay, or wire. Students can bring their dioramas to class for a group viewing or open house.

9

SACRAMENTS

An elderly couple was enjoying an Alaskan cruise, a fiftieth wedding anniversary gift from their children, when the woman suddenly realized that her wedding band was missing. She went into panic mode, trying to remember the last time she had seen it. Was it in the pool or Jacuzzi? Had she left it in a restroom at a port? She asked everyone to search; some children even dove into the pool to try to find the missing treasure. Trying to be reassuring, her husband reminded her that the ring was not very expensive—they couldn't afford much fifty years ago—and he promised a new, lovely ring when they docked.

The woman cried; no other ring could ever be the same! This thin silver band represented fifty years of life together: their initial love that had grown and deepened; the happiness and tribulations of raising their children; the joy of grandchildren; the shared meals and holiday traditions that bound their family together; the little arguments that called for forgiveness; the challenges of illnesses; and the sadness of becoming family elders when their own parents died. That inexpensive ring symbolized their entire journey together as a married couple.

A General Understanding of Sacraments

Like the ring, sacraments are visible signs that point beyond themselves to a greater, invisible reality. But sacraments are more. Sacraments are efficacious signs—they effect or bring about what they symbolize because Christ acts in the sacraments. They freely give grace, a share in the divine life. When we respond to this grace, our union with Christ deepens and increases. Sacraments are encounters with the living God: Father, Son and Spirit.

Liturgical life in the Church centers on the sacraments, which were inaugurated by Christ and given to the Church. Sacraments make use of many symbols, ritual actions, and specific formulas. All of the sacraments include a Liturgy of the Word, and many are celebrated within the Mass. The seven sacraments are:

○ The Sacraments of Initiation: **baptism, confirmation,** and **Eucharist**, which initiate and incorporate persons into the Body of Christ, the Church; strengthen the baptized to carry out the mission of the Christ; and nourish them with the Body and Blood of Christ.
○ The Sacraments of Healing: **penance** and **anointing of the sick**, in which Christ forgives sins and heals and reconciles people to God, to each other, and to the Church.
○ The sacraments at the service of Communion: **matrimony** and **holy orders**, which build up the Church by conferring a special mission to witness and to serve.

As a catechist, you will undoubtedly teach your students about several of the sacraments each year. You may even prepare your young people to celebrate one or more of the sacraments. Your catechesis should always be appropriate to the age and maturity of the students. The sacramental formation you develop will be built on and amplified in succeeding years.

In providing catechesis for the sacraments, you will want to be familiar with the baptismal catechumenate, which has been called the "inspiration for all catechesis" (*NDC* 115). The catechumenate is the process by which the Church initiates adults and unbaptized children who have reached the age of reason.

The catechumenate process fosters lifelong catechesis and includes several rites and rituals. It encompasses four periods:

- **Evangelization**, in which inquiry about the faith and initial conversion takes place;
- **Catechumenate**, devoted to understanding the Sunday readings, to a systematic catechesis, and to discernment of readiness of those preparing for sacraments.
- **Purification**, usually coinciding with Lent, a time of prayer and the Scrutinies in which those who will be initiated are invited to turn from sinfulness and embrace a deeper relationship with the Lord.
- **Mystagogy**, following the reception of the sacraments of initiation, when the newly initiated receive extended catechesis and ongoing formation on living the Christian life.

Allowing the catechumenate to inspire catechesis means that our catechesis encompasses the elements of the process: invitation to conversion, prayer, systematic study of the faith, emphasis on Scripture, ritual, discernment of readiness, ongoing formation, and involvement of the community.

The Sacrament of Baptism

Baptism is the foundational sacrament in which people are initiated and incorporated into the life and mission of the Church. Through immersion or the pouring of water, the initiates die to sin and rise to new life in Christ while the trinitarian formula—"I baptize you in the name of the Father, and of the Son, and of the Holy Spirit"—is prayed. Baptism cleanses original sin and personal sin and grants sanctifying grace, "…a habitual gift of God's own divine life, a stable and supernatural disposition that enables us to live with God and to act by his love" (*USCCA* 514).

The newly baptized person is anointed with sacred chrism (a perfumed oil consecrated by the bishop), sharing in the priesthood of Christ and in his prophetic and royal mission. The usual minister of baptism is a priest or deacon, but anyone can baptize in the case of an emergency. Baptism, the doorway to the other sacraments, imprints an indelible or permanent character and is only received once. But Christians continue to draw on the grace of baptism as they live out their lives in discipleship and mission.

In the Catholic Church, persons are most often baptized as infants, and parents profess their own faith and speak for their child. To help them prepare, parents and godparents receive formation in order to understand the rite of baptism and their responsibilities in raising the child in the faith. It is customary for the candidate for baptism to have at least one godparent, who must be a fully initiated, practicing Catholic, to support them throughout their faith journey.

Adults are initiated into the Catholic faith after lengthy formation in the catechumenate process (the rite of Christian initiation of adults). They receive the sacraments of baptism, confirmation, and Eucharist, normally at the Easter Vigil. Persons baptized in another Christian faith tradition who wish to become Catholic are prepared and received into full communion of the Catholic Church. These persons are not re-baptized, but make a profession of faith and receive confirmation and Eucharist.

The Sacrament of Confirmation

Confirmation deepens the grace of baptism and strengthens the gift of the Holy Spirit that was given initially at baptism. In confirmation, "...wisdom, understanding, counsel, fortitude, knowledge, piety, and fear of the Lord" (*CCC* 1831) are increased, so that those who are confirmed are more firmly rooted in Christ. Confirmation confers the fruits of the Spirit (see Galatians 5:22–23), which empower recipients to carry on the mission of Christ as disciples.

At confirmation, the candidates renew their baptismal vows. The bishop, ordinary minister of confirmation, imposes hands and anoints the candidates with sacred chrism and prays that they will be sealed with the Holy Spirit. Confirmation imprints an indelible character and is received only once.

The Sacrament of the Eucharist

The Eucharist, "...source and summit of the Christian life" (*LG* 11) completes initiation. In the Eucharist, Jesus Christ is really present, wholly and entirely, God and man, under the appearances of bread and wine (see *NDC* 124). The Eucharist is an act of praise and thanksgiving, a sign of unity, and a communion with the Trinity.

Given to the Church at the Last Supper when Christ offered his body and blood to his disciples, the Eucharist is the sacrificial memorial in which Christ's death on the cross is made present. It is a sharing in the life, death and resurrection of Christ and an anticipation of the heavenly banquet. This sacred meal provides nourishment for the Church and strengthens individuals on their lifelong journey of faith. The Eucharist can be received often, even daily, by those who are free from serious sin. Through the Eucharist, venial sins are forgiven and help is provided to avoid serious or mortal sin.

The essential signs of the sacrament of the Eucharist are unleavened wheat bread and wine. Through the power of the Holy Spirit and the words of the eucharistic prayer spoken by the priest, the bread and wine really and substantially become the Body and Blood of Christ. This is called transubstantiation. "When we receive Communion, we need to remember that we are not changing Christ into ourselves. Jesus is transforming us into himself" (*USCCA* 227).

The basic structure of the eucharistic liturgy or the Mass that we celebrate today has remained unchanged since the second century. It consists of introductory rites, the Liturgy of the Word (including readings and homily), the Liturgy of the Eucharist (including preparation of gifts, the eucharistic prayer, and Communion), and concluding rites. We understand that it is our privileged obligation to actively participate in the celebration of Mass each Sunday.

The Sacrament of Penance

Before he ascended into heaven, Jesus gave power to his Apostles to forgive sins and to carry on his ministry of forgiveness. In the sacrament of penance, sins committed after baptism are forgiven, and sinners are reconciled to God. This sacrament emphasizes the unconditional love and mercy of God, who seeks out sinners and draws them to himself like a good shepherd. The sacrament grants forgiveness for personal sin when the penitent expresses sorrow.

Penance is normally celebrated either in an individual rite or a communal rite. Both rites include: a Scripture reading, the individual confession of sins to a priest, a penance (prayer, self-denial, or a work of mercy) given by the priest to the penitent, an expression of sorrow and act of contrition by the penitent, and absolution given by the priest. There are usually several priests available to hear individual confessions at a communal celebration. We are encouraged to receive this sacrament of healing often, especially when we have committed serious sin.

The Sacrament of Anointing of the Sick

In the sacrament of anointing of the sick, the Church continues Christ's healing power and expresses concern for those who are sick in mind, body, or spirit. Any baptized person who is seriously or chronically ill, elderly, or undergoing surgery should receive this sacrament. By the laying on of hands, the anointing with oil, and the prayers of the priest, the sick person is united with the suffering Christ and receives strength. Through this sacrament, which is only administered by bishops or priests, sins are forgiven; physical, mental, and spiritual health may be restored. When a person is dying, the priest administers the last rites, which include penance, anointing, and Eucharist (called *Viaticum,* or food for the journey).

The Sacrament of Matrimony

In matrimony, a baptized man and a baptized woman freely give themselves in a permanent covenant based on the love of Christ and love of each other, expressed in mutual self-giving. In this sacred relationship, couples vow love and fidelity to each other for the length of their lives and willingly accept children as gifts from God. This sacrament, which the bride and groom administer to each other as they exchange vows and rings, establishes a permanent, indissoluble unity. The priest or deacon is the witness for the Church, as couples give their consent in the presence of two additional witnesses and the community.

The Sacrament of Holy Orders

While baptism confers a common priesthood upon all Church members, the Church calls forth some men to receive ministerial priesthood in the sacrament of holy orders. Through the laying on of hands and consecration by a bishop, baptized men are ordained for service to Christ and to his Church in one of three orders: deacon, priest, or bishop. Each order has its particular roles and functions, but all share in the saving action of Jesus through teaching, governing, and sanctifying.

PRACTICAL HELPS FOR THE CATECHIST

Some ways to increase your students' understanding of the important role of sacraments in the life of the Church are:

○ Let young people experience the major sacramental symbols. Bring water, oil, bread, wine (grape juice), and discuss the qualities and everyday uses of these elements. Place older students in groups and have them research and present their symbol to the class.

○ As you study a sacrament, allow children to dramatize it. Assign different roles and include the signs, symbols, and ritual actions of the sacrament.

○ Suggest that parents accompany their children to a celebration of baptism, confirmation, anointing, ordination, or matrimony and discuss what they all observed.

○ Invite families to an upcoming penance celebration and a eucharistic liturgy. Ask parents to help their children learn the Mass responses.

○ Teach students the order of the Mass by creating a game. Write the names of the parts of the Mass (Lord Have Mercy, Gloria, Gospel, etc.) on individual 3x5 cards. Shuffle them, and let students put them in order. Use pictures of the major parts of the Mass for younger children.

○ Use an age-appropriate video of the celebration of sacraments to help students understand the celebration. Make a video of different sacraments being celebrated at your parish.

○ Ask members of the parish community to become prayer partners for students who will be receiving a sacrament this year.

10

DISCIPLESHIP: LIVING LIFE IN CHRIST

Preparing even a small parcel of land for a backyard garden is a daunting task. Knowing the soil consistency and which plants will grow well requires study. Digging and turning over dirt, removing stones, enriching the soil, and planting the seeds are very labor-intensive. Maintaining the garden requires equal dedication and commitment. Watering, plucking weeds, pruning diseased parts, and eliminating detrimental pests during the growing season is arduous work.

Like cultivating a beautiful garden, sustaining our life in Christ requires dedication, commitment, and ardor. Living a moral and virtuous life based on Gospel values bears much fruit, but requires hard work and perseverance. Responding to our call to discipleship involves ongoing conversion, where we strive to cooperate with God's grace, overcome the stumbling block of sin, practice virtue, and eliminate harmful vices. Genuine discipleship entails more than exterior conformity to laws; it requires an interior change of heart and a deliberate endeavor to follow in the footsteps of Christ. Authentic discipleship involves more than knowledge. It demands action.

The Dignity of the Human Person

God created human beings in his own image and likeness, giving us a dignity above any other created things, and destining us for everlasting life. God implanted in our hearts a natural law that "...expresses our human dignity and is the foundation of our basic human rights and duties. This law within us leads us to choose the good that it reveals" (*USCCA* 327). God revealed our integral worth by redeeming us through the life, death, and resurrection of Christ. Christian moral teaching is grounded in the dignity and worth of the human person.

God also gave us free will, the ability to make decisions for good or for evil. Our freedom and dignity come with a moral responsibility to God, to others, and to ourselves. As Christians, the life and teachings of Jesus offer a moral ideal toward which we strive, and present principles that guide our decision-making. Even when our culture militates against the dignity of human life, our decisions and actions should support and uphold the sacredness of life at all stages.

Guides for Christian Living

As disciples, we look to the teachings of Christ and of the Catholic Church to determine how to live a life rooted in Christian moral principles. The Ten Commandments offer a basic understanding of moral living, and should be known and followed. In the Sermon on the Mount (Matthew 5—8), Jesus does not abolish the Commandments but perfects them, indicating that Christian living goes beyond observing laws. Christian living involves selfless living and serving others. A disciple goes the extra mile, loves enemies, and turns the other cheek. The disciple imitates Jesus who models kingdom-living based on the values expressed in the Beatitudes. A disciple prizes meekness, mercy, peace, and poverty in spirit. A disciple thirsts for righteousness and accepts rejection and persecution.

Jesus offers us a new commandment that calls us to love God with our whole being, and to love our neighbor as we love ourselves (see Mark 12:30–31). Jesus gives us a model of servanthood (see John 13:1–17). We will be judged on our care for the hungry, thirsty, or naked (see Matthew 25:31–46).

The Church guides disciples in living out the command to love and serve through the Corporal Works of Mercy—"…to feed the hungry, give drink to the thirsty, shelter the homeless, clothe the naked, visit the sick, visit the prisoners, bury the dead, and give alms to the poor" (*USCCA* 508)—and the Spiritual Works of Mercy "…counseling the doubtful, instructing the ignorant, admonishing the sinner, comforting the sorrowful, forgiving injuries, bearing wrongs patiently, and praying for the living and the dead" (*USCCA* 529).

The Magisterium of the Church provides guidance on how to live a moral life. Interpreting the teachings of Christ, the Magisterium teaches and upholds moral principles through letters and encyclicals, preaching, and catechesis. This teaching office of the Church advises us authoritatively on how to apply moral principles to our daily lives.

Sin Is a Reality

Gifted with free will, we can choose *not* to live as Christ showed us, and *not* to follow the guidance of the Church. Because we have free will, we can turn away from God, we can wound our relationship with God and with our neighbor, we can choose evil over good—we can choose to sin in thought, word, action, or by omission.

We can knowingly decide to commit grave offense against God: mortal sin. "If not repented, it results in a loss of love and God's grace, and merits eternal punishment in hell, that is, exclusion from the Kingdom of God and thus eternal death" (*USCCA* 313). Venial sin is a lesser offense against God. But persistence in venial sin can lead us to a more serious state of sinfulness. When we know that we have sinned, we should rely on God's mercy, express sorrow for our sinfulness, and confess our sins in the sacrament of penance.

Grace and Virtue Are Even Greater Realities

Throughout our lives, God freely and abundantly bestows grace, a share in the divine life that enables and empowers us to act in love. Our acceptance of this gift strengthens virtue and helps us to live life as committed disciples. Human virtues—habits that we acquire through repetition—help us to avoid sin and live morally upstanding lives. To nurture a virtuous life, we repeatedly practice human virtues such as being kind, compassionate, fair, honest, responsible, courageous, and self-disciplined. These virtues, expressed in action, are linked to the four cardinal virtues of justice, prudence, temperance, and fortitude.

The theological virtues—faith, hope, and charity (or love)—are related to God and "…beginning with Baptism, they are infused within us as gifts from God. They dispose us to live in relationship with the Holy Trinity. Faith, hope, and charity influence human virtues by increasing their stability and strength for our lives" (*USCCA* 317).

As disciples, we endeavor to respond to God's grace, and we strive to live virtuous lives so that we might become Christ-like.

The Formation of Conscience

Conscience is the interior sense or ability by which we assess whether an action is right or wrong. A well-formed and enlightened conscience leads us to choose good over evil. Many factors such as age, maturity, and intellectual ability affect the development of an enlightened conscience (see *NDC* 165). But each of us is responsible for developing an informed conscience, for faithfully following our conscience, and for acting on what we know to be good.

The Scriptures, the example of Jesus, the guidance of the Holy Spirit, Church teaching, and the witness of others assist us in our judgments. "The Word of God is a principal shaper of conscience when assimilated by study, prayer, and practice. The prudent advice and good example of others support and enlighten our consciences. The authoritative teaching of the Church is an essential element in our conscience formation" (*USCCA* 320).

As catechists, we have a responsibility to assist our students in forming their consciences. We provide students with opportunities to examine the correctness of actions, to understand their consequences, to make good decisions, and to act on those decisions. We introduce them to Christian witnesses who have made decisions to do good instead of evil. We familiarize our young people with the teachings of the Church, which guide them throughout their lives in making morally correct decisions.

The Social Teachings of the Church

Jesus ministered to the poor, the outcasts, and the disenfranchised members of the society of his day. Today, an integral part of the mission of the Church is to bring the love of Christ to society, to identify injustice in any form, and to work for justice. As leaven in society, Christians have an essential responsibility in carrying out the social mission of the Church by integrating the social teaching of the Church into their lives, and by acting on behalf of justice for the poor and disenfranchised.

Catholic social teaching, promulgated in several important encyclicals and documents, is grounded in the emphatic belief in the dignity of all human beings, and seeks to protect the rights of all human persons. It respects the family as the cornerstone of society, and understands that governments and institutions should use morally acceptable ways to promote the common good. The Church upholds the rights of workers to receive decent wages for their labor, and to work in conditions that respect their human dignity. It teaches that as members of the human community, we are in solidarity with each other, we are interdependent, and we are stewards of God's creation. The Church expresses an option for the poor and speaks out against unjust structures which keep people impoverished.

Social Sin

The emphasis by the Church to promote social justice has led to an understanding of social sin as "…sins that produce unjust social laws and oppressive institutions. They are social situations and institutions contrary to divine goodness" (*USCCA* 528) and are expressed in structures or situations that exploit or oppress people. Some examples are racism, war, slavery, sexism, violence, and discrimination.

Individuals may feel overwhelmed in the face of social sin and social structures that are unjust. However, "[O]ur Gospel commitment to Christ's Kingdom of love, justice, and mercy always includes advocating and supporting fairness for all. God calls us to form community and to correct both the symptoms and causes of injustice that rip apart the solidarity of a community" (*USCCA* 325).

As part of our own ongoing conversion, we must consider areas of change in our own lives, areas where we must root out hatred, exclusivity, prejudicial thinking, or action. We must find situations where we will take positive steps to work for justice and peace, and ways that we can be better stewards of creation. As a community, we need to examine our physical and social environments and determine what action can be taken to change and correct unjust structures or institutions.

Life in Christ Shapes Our Discipleship

Living a life in Christ is our defining role as Christians. "Life in Christ is a way of being, a way of loving....Life in Christ shapes human beings anew and provides a new vital principle for all their activity. It is the radical integration of the person with Christ, the indwelling of Christ in the heart and soul of the Christian, a fusion of the Christian with the Son of God" (*NDC* 183–184). As catechists, we hope to inspire our young people to live the principled life of a disciple of Christ. We assist them in developing well-formed consciences in order that they can make decisions for good rather than evil. We encourage them to express their love for God and their neighbor through service and action.

PRACTICAL HELPS FOR THE CATECHIST

Use a variety of activities to teach your students about living life in Christ:

○ Create individual posters or a wall mural of the Corporal or Spiritual Works of Mercy or the Beatitudes. Let children find pictures, headlines, magazine articles, etc., which illustrate each work or beatitude.

○ Create age-appropriate situations where your students might face a moral problem or dilemma. For example, they have the opportunity to put graffiti on a wall in their neighborhood, or to exclude an ethnically different student from group play. Discuss these situations and the consequences of good and bad decisions. Allow students to see these situations from different perspectives.

○ Encourage students to respect others in the way they speak, pray, play, and act.

○ Raise your students' awareness of their own self-worth. Look at advertisements or commercials. Point out how commercials often lead people to believe that their worth is measured by the things that they have—the shoes or jeans that they wear—rather than the persons they are.

○ Ask parents to help their children memorize the Ten Commandments and the Beatitudes and to learn an Act of Contrition.

○ Give your young people a sense of the global community by using a video showing children from different countries around the world. Attune them to the needs of other people. Your diocesan mission office may be able to assist you with pictures, booklets, or speakers.

○ Occasionally use an age-appropriate examination of conscience as a class prayer. Teach students to examine their consciences each evening; encourage them to include the times they have lived up to their call as Christian disciples, as well as areas where they need improvement.
○ Encourage young people to be stewards of creation by highlighting reduce-reuse-recycle efforts in your area.
○ Help students understand how to resolve difficulties by using peaceful methods of listening and discussion rather than argument and fighting.

11

NOURISHING YOUR CALL
AS A CATECHIST

By now you are aware that the tremendous and wonderful catechetical journey on which you are embarking is a Commitment with a capital "C." In accepting this privileged call as catechist, you understand the need to devote many hours to study, planning, preparation, and teaching. In saying "yes," you have affirmed your desire to share your knowledge and love of God with your students, to share with them the teachings of the Church, and to encourage them to follow Christ as his disciples.

To nourish your own call as a catechist, it is important to take good care of yourself physically and spiritually so that you do not burn out. Maintain a healthy lifestyle in order to have the energy and stamina to teach. If necessary, relinquish one or two other commitments in order to devote the needed time to catechesis. Cultivate your spiritual well-being through daily prayer, Scripture reading, and active participation in the sacramental and community life of your parish.

Continue to nurture your own formation through courses, study, and reading. Take advantage of catechist certification courses if you are able. They provide an excellent foundation for your ministry. If possible, attend diocesan or regional conferences. It is very inspiring and confidence-building to participate in a conference with several hundred catechists who, like you, are enthusiastic about spreading the Good News. When you attend a conference or read a helpful publication, take good notes and refer to them often. Keep a record of your own formation by tracking catechetical events, courses, and workshops that you attend. Many dioceses require this information in order to renew certification.

The longer you serve as a catechist, the more you will uncover a very beautiful facet and blessing of the ministry of catechesis:

The more you give of yourself to form, inform, and transform young people...

...the more you yourself will be formed, informed, and transformed.

As you help your students discover the loving God who always seeks them...

...you yourself will find God.

As you assist your children in experiencing the Christ who came to bring life...

...you too will experience the fullness of life in Christ.

As you encourage your young people to be open to the empowering gifts of the Holy Spirit...

...you will also be empowered.

As you teach your students about how the Church carries on the ministry of Jesus...

...you will become a more dedicated minister.

As you prepare your young people to journey in the promise of Christ to be present until the end of time...

...you will experience the powerful, ever-present Christ on your own life journey.

Bon voyage!

Handbook for Today's Catholic
Revised Edition
ISBN: 978-0- 7648-1220-0

Handbook for Today's Catholic is presented in easy-to-understand language, with content divided into Beliefs, Practices, Prayers, and Living the Faith, and is also fully indexed to the Catechism of the Catholic Church. RCIA and parish adult faith formation groups, high school religious education classes, inquirers into the Catholic Faith, and anyone who wants to have the essentials of Catholicism at their fingertips will welcome this affordable faith resource.

Sharing the Faith With Your Child
From Birth to Age Four
ISBN: 978-0-7648-1523-2

With practical wisdom the authors of this handbook show parents how their daily lives, experiences, and relationships reinforce their role as parents. The book includes chapters on Parenting, Being a Family, Being a Catholic Family, and Rearing Children in a Christian Family.

When's God Gonna Show Up?
Daily Discoveries of the Divine
Marge Fenelon
ISBN: 978-0-7648-1832-5

Written in a warm conversational tone, the stories and reflections in *When's God Gonna Show Up?* draw on the everyday experiences of Marge Fenelon as wife, mother, and Catholic. Entertaining and thought-provoking, her stories lead you to discover God's presence in the small events in your daily life. With humor and grace, these stories will not only entertain you, but will bring you to a new awareness of how God is working in your life.